Selling Swimsuits in the Arctic

Adam Hamilton

with Cynthia Gadsden

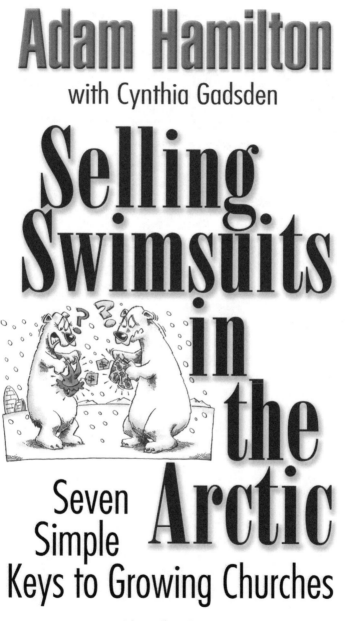

Selling Swimsuits in the Arctic

Seven Simple Keys to Growing Churches

Abingdon Press
Nashville

SELLING SWIMSUITS IN THE ARCTIC
SEVEN SIMPLE KEYS TO GROWING CHURCHES

This book is printed on acid-free paper.

Library of Congress Cataloging-in-Publication Data

Hamilton, Adam, 1964-
    Selling swimsuits in the arctic : seven simple keys to growing churches / Adam Hamilton and Cynthia Gadsden.
        p. cm.
    ISBN 0-687-34384-4 (pbk. : alk. paper)
    1. Church marketing.   2. Church growth.   I. Gadsden, Cynthia.   II. Title.
    BV652.23.H36 2005
    254'.5—dc22
                                                                    2005005227

05 06 07 08 09 10 11 12 13 14—10 9 8 7 6 5 4 3
MANUFACTURED IN THE UNITED STATES OF AMERICA

This book is dedicated to the pastors and lay leaders of the churches in the former Soviet Union who face very difficult challenges with courage as they seek to develop vibrant congregations. They are among my heroes in the faith.

Contents

Introduction

Why is it that some businesses fail and some succeed? Though I am a pastor I find the world of business to be a refreshing place to go to study the dynamics of human organizations and the lessons for success and failure that are often missed in the church world. Every business must get certain things right if it will succeed. If the business fails to grasp the lessons of this book, it will fail. I believe the same is true of the church.

I am not proposing that starting new churches and growing existing churches is simply a matter of doing the things listed in this little book. But I am suggesting that if you don't do these seven things, it will be almost impossible to see your church grow.

The ideas in this book are simple. There's nothing in here that you do not already know. But sometimes naming the obvious is important.

This book was conceived late one night, after four days of teaching and conversations with pastors of struggling churches in Russia. I had met with 110 pastors and church leaders and listened to their stories of frustration. Many of these churches had been in existence for several years and still only had ten to twenty people attending worship. Some were already experiencing decline. The pastors wanted to see their churches be healthy and vital places of worship, evangelism, and community transformation. But in many of their congregations things were not going well.

It was at the end of this conference, as I met with one more pastor and her husband, sitting at their kitchen table in Siberia, that I felt led to set out the ideas in this book. It seemed clear to me that these ideas were the starting point for addressing the frustrations of these churches and the keys to developing vital congregations.

In the former Soviet Union, church leaders, having grown up under socialism, are just learning about how a free-market system operates. Growing up there were very few choices people could make for themselves regarding goods and services—the government dictated what people would wear, what food would be available in the stores, what people would buy. Under this kind of system sales and marketing were not necessary. Quality of goods and services was notoriously poor as there were no competitive market forces requiring constant improvement. There was little incentive for manufacturers to understand the needs and desires of the market—instead the market (the people) modified their needs and desires to match the goods and services the government decided to produce.

But all of this has changed. Today the successful companies in the former Soviet Union are learning to produce goods and services people want, with a quality they recognize and at a price they can afford. New products require the use of effective marketing, including market research and advertising, in order to induce potential customers to try them. If the products deliver on their promises and enhance the quality of life of the customer, the customer will continue to buy, and he or she will tell others about the product.

These have been hard lessons for businesses to learn in the former Soviet countries, but those who have learned them have been rewarded. What struck me as I visited churches in Russia is that those churches headed by pastors who learned these lessons were thriving. But those churches that did not understand some of the basic principles of a free market were struggling. And then it dawned on me—things are not so different for the churches in the United States. We have emerged from what once was a predominantly Christian society where being a part of a church was assumed and where Christian ideals and values were sometimes explicitly, and certainly implicitly, accepted in society. But today we live in a post-Christian culture where the church is now forced to compete with a host of other activities and organizations for the interest, involvement, time, and resources of people. In addition, for mainline churches, over the last forty years we've seen the rise of tens of thousands of new "non-denominational" churches, many of which are growing while our congregations continue to decline. We find ourselves in need of learning how to compete in a free-market society.

And this is my reason for writing this book. My hope is to offer a handful of basic principles that are essential to success in nearly any venture. These principles are true for churches and for individual ministries within those churches. The lessons are important for lay leaders, staff, and clergy. Do these things and you are likely to see a growing organization. Ignore them, and you will likely oversee the decline of your ministry, program, or church.

This book is written to be read in one sitting—you can read it in thirty minutes. It is written to be read by lay people, by church staff members, and by pastors. The lessons in it are as valuable for a specific ministry area or group in the church as they are for the church as a whole. It will be most effective when used as the basis of discussion for members of your leadership team or staff, whether you are a pastor or the leader of a Sunday school class you hope to see become more vital or the director of a ministry area in the church.

To illustrate the seven leadership principles outlined in this book I have offered you a story—not of a pastor, but a salesman. I have intentionally stepped outside the church world, and utilized sales and marketing terminology. I have done so because I often find it helpful to look at what we do in the church from the perspective of those outside the church. The terms themselves help us see what we do in a new light. In the opening chapter I will make the point that church leadership is all about sales— we're selling ideas, attempting to persuade persons to commit their time, talent, and resources in service to Christ and through the ministry of our church. You may feel uncomfortable using sales and marketing terms for what we do in the church; feel free to substitute your own more traditional theological or ministry terms, but don't miss the ideas—they are the keys to developing churches and ministries that are successfully reaching new people for Christ.

With this in mind, let's get started . . .

CHAPTER ONE

It's All Sales

I would like to introduce you to a great guy named Bob. Bob works in sales, and sells swimsuits, of all things—men's swimsuits, women's swimsuits, even children's swimsuits. He represents one of the leading swimsuit manufacturers in the world—and he sells his wares to big department stores as well as small boutiques. And he's very good at what he does. In this little book we're going to learn seven important lessons from Bob that will help us in our work in the church. But before we look at Bob's intriguing tale, let's get one thing straight—*it's all sales*. Virtually everything we do in life can be looked at as a form of sales.

Some folks have a negative connotation of salespeople. Certainly comparing church ministry to sales will seem to some crass and to others nearly sacrilegious. But the truth is there is a great deal about leading churches and ministries, as well as many other areas of life, that involve sales.

Consider these examples. Every time that you have applied for a job you were involved in sales. The product you were selling was yourself and your marketing tools were a resumé and cover letter. Your sales presentation was your interview. Your aim was to help the interviewer to understand why, of the twenty applicants, you might be best for the job. Those who can sell themselves best typically get the best jobs.

Or consider your local congressman or congresswoman. In order to get elected she (or he) has to convince the voters that she is the right person for the job; we know this involves sales and marketing—we see it in television commercials and flyers mailed to our home. But her sales job is not finished when she is elected—in a sense it is just getting started. For every piece of legislation she sponsors, she must be able to convince her fellow legislators to support it. This too is sales.

Great teachers understand this as well. When a teacher stands before a class of twenty-five sixteen-year-olds to teach history or chemistry or composition, he can simply present the material and hope for the best. But the really great teachers know that they must sell their students on the importance of history or chemistry or composition. Their enthusiasm for the subject, their ability to demonstrate the importance of this subject for sixteen-year-old students, will determine how many students look forward to attending class, consider a career in this field, and actively pursue their studies.

When I was in college I worked for a department store selling women's shoes. Go ahead, laugh if you like, but it was a great job! One day I was waiting upon a woman looking for a pair of shoes to wear to a special event, when an older gentleman came and sat down to rest in one of the chairs in my department. I didn't think much about this—men routinely came and sat down in our chairs waiting for their wives to finish their shopping. I continued to wait upon my customer, helping her find the perfect shoe for her dress.

In selling women's shoes I came to understand that I had to help each woman find the right shoe—but that was only half the job. I also wanted to know my shoes so well that I could help each woman feel great about the shoes she was buying. Finally, I wanted to help the woman have a great experience buying the shoes, knowing that if she had a wonderful experience, she would likely become a repeat customer. I knew salespeople who simply brought out whatever shoes a woman pointed to and quietly sat there while she tried them on, waiting to see if she decided to purchase them. But I tried to understand what the woman's needs were, why she was looking for shoes, and what she valued most in her footwear. I would suggest certain shoes and tell her about the material they were made from, how they were styled, and why they were terrific shoes. I believed in the products we sold.

On this particular day I brought out to my customer a beautiful pair of calfskin pumps that fit her needs perfectly. I described how these shoes were made, the quality of the leather, and the elegance of the style. She tried them on and they fit like a glove. Not only did they fit well, they looked great. My only comment was, "Now that's a pair of shoes!" With genuine enthusiasm she said, "I'll take them!" I responded, "You are going to love these shoes. If you are interested, I have the matching purse here, made of the same leather and designed by the same designer, would you like to see it?" "Of course!" she replied. Soon this woman left with a great pair of shoes, a beautiful purse, and a real excitement about wearing her new shoes to her upcoming event. I sat down quickly after the sale, as I did with every pair of shoes I sold, and wrote her a thank-you note, expressing gratitude that she allowed me to help her with her shoe needs.

When I came back out to the sales floor the older gentleman was still sitting there in his chair and he finally spoke to me, saying, "Son, my name is Alfred Leightner, do you know who I am?" My heart nearly stopped—this was the CEO of the company! "Yes, sir, you are the head of our company—it's a pleasure to meet you," I said, terrified that the head of the company had been sitting in my department watching me for the last fifteen minutes. He spoke again and said, "You are an incredible salesman, young man. You've got a great future ahead of you with our company." To which I instinctively replied, "Thank you, Mr. Leightner, but I am studying in college to be a pastor—I guess I intend to sell a different product. I am devoting my life to helping others see why they need Christ and convincing them to commit their lives to him!"

I don't think I understood at the time just how apt this metaphor was in capturing the work I do in the church. Over the last twenty years, serving in multiple roles in four different churches, there is not one position I've held in the church that did not involve sales in order to be successful.

As a youth pastor, associate minister, and founding pastor of a new church, I've spent the last twenty years in sales. In devising strategies to reach teenagers and persuade them to follow Christ, in reaching out to new visitors to the church, in teaching Bible studies in which I sought to encourage people to actually live what the Bible was teaching, in ministering to people in the hospital, seeking to help them find peace before surgery, and in starting a new congregation, trying to persuade people to become a part of a church that had no building, no established programs, and no history, I was pursuing my work in sales.

I've come to see that every sermon I preach is, in a way, a sales presentation. I am trying to convince a congregation of people of their need for the particular spiritual truth lifted up in the scripture passage of the day and then to motivate and inspire them to actually do something in response to the word. My invitation at the end of the sermon is my attempt to "close the sale" each week.

Regardless of your area of leadership or ministry in the church, you are in sales. The women's group wants to attract younger women to their programs—this will involve sales. The youth group needs additional adult sponsors—this will involve sales. The congregation desperately wants to reach out to its community and bring in unchurched people, helping them become authentic Christians—this involves sales.

Unfortunately, few seminaries offer basic training in sales. I have yet to see a continuing education event for pastors and church leaders focused on improving sales skills (Church of the Resurrection's annual Leadership Institute does include a focus in this area). And this is why I've written this book. Not to be a complete guide to sales, but to get you started thinking about some of the most basic questions in sales, and the most fundamental principles, in the hope that you will see something about your work as a church leader, or perhaps about the product you are selling (Christianity, the church, or a particular ministry in the church), that you had not seen before.

By way of illustrating these principles, I'd like to return to the story of Bob, our swimsuit salesman. Bob is an outstanding salesman—very successful at what he does. People all over the Southeast wear his swimsuits. But what would happen if Bob left the warmth of the Southeast and took his product line to the coldest place in the United States? Throughout this book we'll follow Bob's attempts to sell swimsuits in the Arctic.

Bob and his wife, Allison, are headed for their new home in Alaska's northernmost city, Barrow, by small bush plane. For five years Bob has been a top salesman for SecondSkin, a swimsuit manufacturer on the Florida Gulf Coast. Now though, encased in the latest beat-the-wind-and-cold outerwear, Bob is still a bit stunned by the whirlwind changes in their lives.

Allison, newly armed with a doctorate in linguistics, received word just weeks ago that she was one of five people to receive the Creekinhot Fellowship, the most prestigious grant in linguistics in the world. The money will allow her to continue her research on the native languages spoken in the Arctic. Barrow has the largest concentration in North America of the Inupiat, the name they prefer instead of Eskimos, and are the people many consider the first inhabitants of North America.

"But how are you going to sell swimsuits there?" Bob's buddies at work had asked when they heard the news.

"Just imagine all the folks up there who don't know about our suits. It's truly uncharted territory," he'd replied. "I just see myself as going to open up the territory for us."

They had looked at each other and laughed. Bob was nothing if not optimistic. He was one of those people who never saw a half-empty glass, only one that wasn't full yet. One year after the worst hurricane in Florida's history and an unprecedented rainy spell in the rest of the U.S., Bob had showed up at their national sales meeting in the latest SecondSkin swim trunks, tank top, sunglasses, and flip-flops. His hair was gelled, and he'd even applied sunscreen on his nose for the occasion. Outside the meeting, a flash flood was in full force, while inside spirits were pretty low about the coming selling season. That had all changed as Bob walked to the podium. In response to the laugher and catcalls, Bob had said,

"I know my outfit seems a bit funny, today in particular, but you know when it's pouring outside I get excited. Know why? Because I know that pretty soon it's going to be hot and steamy, and then I'm going to sell lots of swimsuits. I know a good, long dry spell is always just around the corner. I just have to hang on till it gets here.

"When it's hot outside I know I'm going to sell lots of swimsuits, because people will want them in several colors. When it's cold outside, I don't worry because warm weather is only days away, and I know I'm going to sell a lot of swimsuits. When a store manager says no to carrying our suits, or tries to convince me another product is better, I say, 'Now this is good, but have you seen this?' Then I show 'em what our product has to offer, and I know that once they see what we have I'm going to sell a lot of swimsuits."

Bob had continued like that for another ten minutes, and got a cheering ovation when he finished. The featured speaker got up, went to the mike, and said, "Ditto," then sat down. From that day on, Bob was known as the guy who could sell swimsuits in the rain.

Now, watching the earth from the small plane, Bob saw the landscape change from urban, to lush green, and finally to frozen white desert. The irony of moving to a place where in summer the sun doesn't set for eighty-four days, but where it's still too cool for swimwear, wasn't entirely lost on Bob. He knew selling swimsuits up here would be difficult, but he had overcome obstacles before. And he was the kind of guy who loved a good challenge. Yet as he looked out his window on the snow-covered earth below, even he was beginning to wonder whether it was really possible to sell swimsuits in the Arctic.

Questions for Reflection

1. In what ways is "sales" a part of what we do as leaders? As the church?

2. How is a sermon like a sales presentation?

3. Describe a salesperson you have found effective.

4. What kind of salesperson repels you?

Seven Keys to Success in Sales

Afterr college, Bob decided to pursue a career in sales. A mentor and friend told him that he had the gifts and graces for such a career. The first sales job he received after school was working as a rep for a swimsuit distributor. He was assigned a territory in Florida, near the Gulf Coast, and he routinely called upon the clothing stores in this territory, speaking to the various buyers for these stores and seeking to encourage them to purchase his line of swimsuits.

In order to succeed at this job Bob quickly discovered seven important keys to sales:

1. He must believe in his product. If he didn't believe his swimsuits were the finest available—that they offered the best value and the most attractive styling—he would never be able to convince others to purchase them.

2. He must believe that people need his product. Bob had to believe that the lives of his customers would be enhanced by what he was selling. He knew that people like to swim, and that when they swim they don't want to feel self-conscious or unattractive—and thus he believed that his product was an important one to sell. He could help people feel better about themselves and enhance their ability to enjoy life by selling them his swimsuits. This conviction,

coupled with his belief in the quality of his company's swimsuits, gave Bob a passion that is important in sales.

3. He must understand the needs of his customers. *Bob had a large line of swimsuits he could sell, at every different price point and style. He knew that people needed swimsuits, but different people had different needs when it came to swimsuits. For some buyers the most important consideration was price. For competitive swimmers the need was for suits that had low resistance in water. For some, purchasing a swimsuit was a terrifying proposition each year, and they needed swimwear that would help them not feel overly self-conscious about their figure. Still others wanted the latest styles and fashions. Of the vast number of possible swimsuits he could sell to a department store, Bob came to realize that his first task was to understand the needs of his customers—in this case the buyers of the department stores and their primary base of consumers. If he didn't understand their needs and goals in the area of swimsuit sales, if he didn't understand the customers they were seeking to reach, he would have a tough time selling his suits.*

4. He must offer an excellent product. *Bob knew that while it is possible to sell a product to a buyer once, only a product that actually delivered on its promises would see the kind of repeat business necessary for success.*

5. He must embody the product. *This may sound a bit strange, but Bob came to understand that sales is, in large part, about building relationships and building trust. Buyers in department stores would formulate their views about Bob's swimsuits in large part based upon their impressions of Bob himself. If Bob was warm, enthusiastic, honest, and sharp, his potential customers would associate his products with these attributes. But if Bob was rude, unprofessional, dishonest, or uninformed, they would associate his products with these attributes. Bob had to embody the values of his company and his product line.*

6. He must effectively market the product. *Bob knew that once he had the right product, and he had the product right, he would need to effectively tell the story of his product to others. He would need to sell not only the buyers for the department store, but he would also need to help the salespeople, and even satisfied customers, to be able to sell his products to others. If he did not do this, no matter how wonderful his swimsuits might be, they would simply sit on the shelf.*

7. Bob learned that perseverance was the key to success in sales. *Most department store buyers were not interested in his product line at first—at times it took him six or seven sales calls before the department store buyer would finally decide to carry Bob's line of swimsuits. His mantra came to be the well-worn phrase, "If at first you don't succeed, try, try again!" Bob's success came because he refused to give up.*

Bob learned these lessons well, and he became a great salesman. Buyers in the department stores not only purchased his products, the salespeople talked his swimsuits up among their customers. And because the swimsuits really were terrific, the customers told their friends. And these friends came to the stores asking for SecondSkin's brand of swimsuit.

That's all very interesting, you might say, but what does Bob's story have to do with you and with growing churches and ministries? How does his experience and the secrets of his success relate to your work in the church? Take a few minutes to draw your own parallels and conclusions.

Questions for Reflection

1. What is the product or products that you are selling as a leader in the church? Do you believe in your product? Why?

2. Do people need your product? Why? How will their lives be enriched by availing themselves of this "product"? I have suggested in my book *Leading Beyond the Walls* that there are three questions every church must answer: "Why do people need Jesus Christ?" "Why do they need the church?" and "Why do they need our particular church?" If you are a leader of a ministry area in your church you might ask why people need your particular ministry.

3. Who are your potential customers? What are their needs that your product may help meet? How can you tailor your product to better meet their needs?

4. Is your product built or executed with excellence? After trying your product once do "customers" return?

5. In what ways do you embody your product? What impressions do others gather of your product by watching you? What kind of attributes do others see in you that would draw them to want to "purchase" your "product"? Are there any things you do, or attributes about you, that would repel potential "customers"?

6. Are the people currently involved in your ministry or church equipped and inspired to "sell" your product to their friends and neighbors? Do they believe in the product? Do they represent your ministry well? What are you doing to get the word out to potential "customers" about your product?

7. Do you give up at the first sign of failure, or are you doggedly perseverant in your approach to ministry? When one strategy doesn't succeed, do you quit, or do you look for new strategies for accomplishing your mission?

These questions will help you think about your work in the church and your personal leadership style. The following chapters will examine in more detail these seven keys that are essential for any church or ministry to succeed. We'll do this by following Bob as he faces some difficult decisions in his sales career.

Do *I* Believe in the Product?

Bob had a passion for *SecondSkin* swimsuits. He loved the company, believing that it was a company that was managed with integrity, had great corporate values, and, most important, offered the best product in the marketplace at a reasonable price. He had studied the competition, he understood the market, and he believed in his product. He was so passionate about *SecondSkin* that his wife, Allison, would occasionally have to gently tap him on the leg when they were at supper with friends—a secret code that meant, "Honey, you're talking too much about swimsuits, let's change topics or let someone else talk!" Everyone who knew Bob knew that part of the reason he was so successful at what he did was that he was passionate about his product.

A pastor, Sunday school teacher, or ministry leader who feels this kind of passion about their church or program has already taken the most important step toward success in growing their ministry. We must believe in the product we're selling.

As church leaders we are usually "selling" more than one product. Ultimately we are seeking to lead people to become committed followers of Jesus Christ. If we are to meet with any success at this, we have to personally believe that following Jesus Christ is the most important thing we can do with our lives. We cannot convince others unless we ourselves are convinced of the importance of following Christ. Our ability to be effective Christian leaders is tied to our own commitment to Christ and how well we are tending to our spiritual lives. One of my seminary professors once noted, "You cannot lead people where you yourself are not going."

We must be able to articulate our own spiritual passion. In some cases, we must rediscover that passion. You may have been a Christian for decades, and over time perhaps you've not given enough attention to your spiritual life. Over time our faith can grow lukewarm, our spiritual passion can subside, and we end up in something of a spiritual "rut."

Here I am reminded of the church of Ephesus in our New Testament. Paul spent more than two years in this place, and amazing wonders occurred while he was there. His ministry had led many to a radical commitment to Jesus Christ so that the entire city was experiencing the effects of his preaching. Even the economy was affected, as people burned their magic books and no longer purchased the silver figurines of the goddess Artemis. It is likely that Ephesus became the western center of Christianity for several decades before Rome claimed this honor. Even John the apostle is said to have settled in Ephesus. Tradition has it that Mary the mother of Jesus lived there for a time.

But by the end of the New Testament era, just thirty years after Paul's ministry there, Jesus had this to say to the church of Ephesus:

> "I know your works, your toil and your patient endurance. I know that you cannot tolerate evildoers; you have tested those who claim to be apostles but are not, and have found them to be false. I also know that you are enduring patiently and bearing up for the sake of my name, and that you have not grown weary. But I have this against you, that you have abandoned the love you had at first. Remember then from what you have fallen; repent, and do the works you did at first. If not, I will come to you and remove your lampstand from its place, unless you repent." (Revelation 2:2-5)

There have been many times in the last twenty years of ministry when I have "abandoned" my "first love." I allowed my times

of prayer to grow shorter and shorter. I had been too busy to listen for God's voice through reading the scriptures. I had watched
my faith grow cold.

When this happens, ministry is no longer a joy, but a burden.
I find my preaching lacks power at these times. And I feel like I
am merely going through the motions of ministry.

I believe this happens to every Christian at times. The Hebrew
Bible is the story of a never-ending cycle of God's people aban-
doning their first love and allowing sin and idolatry to sneak into
their corporate life together, eventually leading to devastating
consequences, which sends them back on their knees before God.
God faithfully delivers his people. Their faith is renewed, and
they walk faithfully before the Lord for a season before they grad-
ually begin to fall away once more.

I see this same trend in my marriage. Over the last twenty-two
years, I have fallen in and out of love with my wife several times.
There are times when I am passionately in love with her. But
there have been times when I have felt nothing—when I was
simply going through the motions of being married to her. The
key to rediscovering my first love for her begins with my decision
that I don't want to simply go through the motions of marriage. I
do not want to be satisfied with this—I want something more.

I have found the following things helpful in rekindling my love
for my wife: I begin by praying for her. I spend time speaking with
God, asking God to fill my heart with a love for her. I then begin
giving thanks for her—recalling the blessing she is in my life, I
thank God for her. These words of gratitude lead to *feelings* of
gratitude for her. I then begin focusing on doing loving things
toward her—I seek to bless her. Finally, I seek to spend more
quality time with her. In the end, I rediscover "the love I had at
first" for her.

The same principles work in reclaiming my spiritual passion. I
must spend time in prayer, speaking with God and thanking God
for what God has done for me and for who God is. I reflect upon
the Psalms and I remember and thank God for what God has
done in my life over the years. I look for ways to express my love
for God in service. And I seek to spend more quality time with

God, sometimes taking a personal retreat—time away for nothing but prayer, worship, and scripture study.

I am reminded of the story of the Brooklyn Tabernacle as Jim Cymbala assumed the role of pastor in this church. The congregation had been in decline for years. The first step in the church's renewal was the spiritual revival of its members, which began when the church became serious about prayer.

There is no shortcut to growing healthy churches or vital programs or ministries. We cannot bypass this first step. We have to rediscover our passion for Christ—to reclaim "the love you had at first."

Take a moment here, right now, to write down on a sheet of paper the difference Jesus Christ has made in your life. Consider what your life would have been like apart from him. Describe the blessings that have come as a result of your faith. And then conclude by writing down why you believe others need Jesus Christ in their lives. If you are studying this little book as a group, you might want to plan time to allow your group to discuss these answers and share your personal testimonies regarding the difference Christ has made in your lives.

Each member of your leadership team in your church and your specific ministry area should be able to answer these questions, and not only to answer them, but be passionate about their answers. This is the first step in developing healthy, vital congregations—developing leaders with vital spiritual lives who are passionate about their faith.

Bob leaned back in his seat, thinking about the new line of swimsuits that was coming out next week. He loved this time of year. He couldn't wait for the new swimsuits to arrive. He would spend hours studying the products, the new materials, and the patterns. He would order samples of all of the new men's suits in his own size, and wear them around the house. He'd even take them into the bathtub to see how they fit when wet.

Poor Allison was subjected to the same experience—she would have to try on the different suits, telling Bob which ones she was most excited about and why. And after a week of studying these new suits, and experiencing them for himself, he was ready to call upon the buyers of the various department stores and specialty boutiques across his territory. He always did so with a passion, excited to show his new wares.

As the pilot announced that their plane was preparing to land at the Wiley Post–Will Rogers International Airport, Bob realized that this year would be unlike any other. He would be seeking to sell swimsuits in a land he'd never been to before. He believed he was ready for the challenge.

Questions for Reflection

1. Over time our convictions, our faith, our spiritual passion can become diminished—this is true even for pastors and church leaders. Have you or your church ever experienced what the people of Ephesus had experienced as described in the book of Revelation?

2. Would you describe your congregation, or those in your ministry area, as passionate about your ministry? Their faith? If not, what will it take to help them rediscover their "first love"—to rekindle a spiritual passion?

CHAPTER FOUR

Do Others Need What I'm Selling?

Bob and Allison were quick to settle into their small home in Barrow, Alaska. Allison began her study of Inupiat language and culture with an excitement Bob had never seen before. And Bob began to survey the landscape of his new sales territory, a thriving metropolis of four thousand people—none of whom, he was certain, had swimsuits.

As he began walking down the gravel streets of downtown Barrow, Bob suddenly had the keen awareness that he had entered a world he had never known before. His first clue was the warning he was given by a local who told him, "Whatever you do, please don't feed the polar bears! We're trying to keep them out of town." Surveying the city he came to a large, relatively new building locals called the "AC Value Center"—short for Alaska Commercial. This was the lone "supermarket" in town and the only thing resembling a mall. It was filled with groceries and a host of other items for sale. Bob assessed that this might be his biggest, and perhaps only, account. It was time to break the ice, so to speak!

As he entered the store, he asked the first clerk he met, "Do you carry swimsuits?" The clerk looked a bit confused. "I don't think so. Not in a place that's this cold! People would never wear them." "But you've got the ocean right here—and I've heard you have twenty-four hours of sunshine for days on end. I've even heard it can reach 80 *degrees here in the summer. Surely people would buy swimsuits! Especially if they knew about SecondSkin's swimsuits." Without realizing it, Bob was busy expounding to the clerk the wonders of SecondSkin's suits and their line of new suits aimed to "flatter any figure." Finally, when he paused for a breath, the clerk spoke up, "But sir, the average temperature during the summer is only 40 degrees! And while, on very rare occasions, the temperature has reached 80, that almost never happens. Our people don't need swimsuits, they need coats!"*

And with that Bob was struck by the reality of the situation—did people really need what he was selling? He wasn't questioning whether people needed clothing, nor even if they needed some kind of clothing to wear when getting in the water. But he was beginning to question whether they needed the kind of clothing he was selling.

It was good that Bob was wrestling with this question. It is the kind of question we in the church need to wrestle with from time to time. In the last chapter we considered how Christ makes a difference in our lives. We believe that others need Christ as well. Christians also believe that people need the church. The church is the body of Christ—it is a community of people gathered to worship God, to proclaim and celebrate the good news of Jesus Christ, to grow in faith, to minister to, strengthen, and care for one another, and to serve God together in the world. But the fact that people need Christ and the church does not necessarily mean that they need our particular church, or our ministry or program.

This leads to an important question for church leaders to ask: Do I have the right product for this market? Bob was coming to realize that he may have the best of intentions, and he may be a great salesman, but he may have the wrong product for the people of Barrow, Alaska.

The right product is one that people will buy. It is one that people can ultimately be convinced that they need—or, if not need, that they will come to want, believing it will enhance their quality of life. And it is one that will be economically viable.

In the consumer marketplace a great product does, in fact, improve and enhance the quality of life of potential customers. It adds value. It meets perceived wants or, better yet, real needs. At some point in the future the operation of the business or the sale of the product will produce enough revenue to offset initial start-up costs and sustain the costs of operating while providing some reasonable return on the investment (in the case of the church or a non-profit this return will be used to develop or expand the ministry, to reach new people, or to help fund other mission or ministry ventures outside the walls of the start-up church).

One of the exciting things about the church is that, done well and rightly understood, it is a product that people will always need. Having said that, it is possible that the market for your product has already been saturated by others offering the same or similar products. If this is the case, the only way you will see your business thrive is if you can offer a better product than your competitors.

Several years ago three movie theatres opened within three miles of one another in my community with a total of forty-two screens where previously there had been none. The first two opened within a few months of each other. One felt a bit more elegant. The other a bit "louder" and youth oriented. Both offered average service and similar ticket prices. One had a slightly better location than the other. My wife and I love to go to the movies and we were thrilled to have two theatres—twenty-two new screens—fifteen minutes closer to our home than the next closest theatres. With similar prices, similar films, and similar service, the theatre that felt a bit more sophisticated, which also happened to have a slightly better location, had the competitive advantage. The other theatre began to struggle a bit.

A year later the third theatre opened—a twenty-screen cinema with what was then a new design feature for movie theatres: stadium seating. The seats were more comfortable, the theatres were more elegant, the sound system was more powerful, the service was significantly better, and the overall experience was noticeably superior to the movie-going experience at the other two theatres. Within two years both of the other theatres were out of business.

The cinema market was saturated before the third movie theatre moved into the area, but they opened offering a better product—one that people noticed and told their friends about.

What does this mean for your church? It means that in today's environment, when those looking for a church "shop around," there should be something that stands out about your congregation or your ministry—something that sets you apart. Currently, if someone in your community decided to find a church home, and he or she visited every church in your community, what reasons would this individual have for choosing your congregation? If there are no reasons why they would choose your church, it's time you began focusing on two or three things that you will do well—that will set you apart and would be reasons for someone to make your church their church home.

When we started the church I pastor, The United Methodist Church of the Resurrection in Leawood, Kansas, there were already more than twenty other churches that had started in this community. They were meeting in schools and storefronts and some already had their own buildings. While there were plenty of people moving into or living in this community to support another church, I had to seriously consider why we should start another new church in this community and, just as important, how our church would be different from the others. If we were simply offering the same thing others were offering, perhaps there was neither the need nor the support for another new church.

We found that a majority of the new churches starting in this community were conservative theologically, and stylistically they were offering "contemporary" worship, many patterning their ministry after the wildly successful Willow Creek Community Church outside of Chicago, Illinois. With this in mind we felt there was room for a church that was moderate theologically and offered worship that had a more traditional and slightly liturgical flavor. We would offer our worship with excellence and seek to connect both Word and worship with the everyday lives of the people in our community. Ultimately this was part of the reason for our success—we offered the right product for this particular market, and a product no one was offering in quite this same way. We sought to offer our worship with excellence and relevance.

We believed that people needed this kind of church—that if we did this well, we could reach people no other church was reaching, and we would see their lives transformed as they became followers of Jesus Christ. Ultimately we knew that if their lives were transformed, these persons would live their faith in such a way that the community would be changed.

Bob came to see that the people of Barrow needed clothing, perhaps even clothing to get wet in, but they did not need the kind of swimwear worn on the beaches of south Florida. He was in a place of great need, but he had the wrong product.

One last word about the right product. Once Bob came to understand that the people of Barrow didn't need swimsuits, he had to decide if it was his calling to sell swimsuits, or to sell clothing that the people needed. If what really excited him was selling swimsuits, then he'd have to wait until Allison was finished with her work so he could move to where it was warm. But if what Bob really loved was helping people, then his task was to figure out what the people of Barrow needed or might want, and change his product altogether.

Questions for Reflection

1. What does this mean for your church, ministry, or program? Are you offering what people need, or simply what you want? Are you doing church in a way that would draw people to your congregation, or in a way that is most comfortable for you or your members, or which requires the least effort? Bob had made a critical decision. He would seek to understand the needs of the people he was living among, and develop a product that would meet those needs.

2. One place where many churches wrestle with these kinds of questions is regarding worship styles. How does this chapter

relate to the question of worship styles? In what way are your ministries shaped by the needs of your community and the people God has called you to reach?

3. What are the unmet needs in your community that your church or ministry might seek to meet?

CHAPTER FIVE
Getting the *Right* Product

B
ob spent the next month getting to know the people of Barrow, and not only the folks who lived in the city, but the Inupiat people that Allison had come to study. He learned that Barrow is among the oldest continuously inhabited cities in North America, with a population that can be traced back to as early as A.D. 500. Allison taught him about the important role that the spring whaling season plays among the Inupiat and for the people of Barrow. Together they learned about life in a place where for two months every winter the sun never shines, and where for eighty-four straight days each summer the sun never sets. They learned of life in the oil fields and on the fishing boats. Among the things they learned was that obesity was on the rise, especially among the native people, due to decreasing amounts of exercise and changing dietary habits introduced by those migrating to Barrow.

As Bob learned about the people of Barrow and the North Slope, he kept asking himself, What do the people of the North Slope need that my company could produce? He thought about this long and hard—if he could design the right product, and it could sell in Barrow, it could sell in thousands of cities in northern climates. Suddenly SecondSkin would be a household name for people who live in cooler climates.

Bob began to think of the broader mission of SecondSkin. They created clothing for people to wear outdoors—clothing that was worn when people were active—clothing that was worn by people who sought to use swimming as a means of exercise. He began to consider the kind of clothing people would need in Barrow that would encourage *exercise: clothing that would retain warmth; but unlike the bulky winter clothing most in Barrow were used to—clothing difficult to exercise in—SecondSkin could create clothing so impenetrable to cold, yet so thin and comfortable, that joggers could jog, hikers could hike, and walkers could walk on all but the coldest days.*

Before long Bob had a team of designers from SecondSkin flying into Barrow to catch his vision for this new line of active wear. Allison arranged for Bob and his team to meet with the Inupiat elders, where he would seek their permission to develop a special line of clothing aimed at encouraging the Inupiat—and the other residents of Barrow and the North Slope region—to exercise, and by doing so, to significantly reduce the risk of serious illness that was beginning to threaten their people.

We pastors and church leaders could learn a thing or two from Bob. Often we insist on selling swimsuits in the Arctic, when what the people really need is something entirely different. Our swimsuits are our "sacred cows"—those programs, ministries, or ways of doing church that we're comfortable with, but that may not speak to or reach twenty-first-century people. Our task, if we are to develop churches and ministries that are growing and life transforming, is to understand the needs of the people with whom we seek to minister.

It strikes me that Jesus provides us a wonderful example here. He didn't simply come preaching the kingdom of God (which was his passion, and his central message), he also came meeting the needs of people. In the Gospels Jesus is continually healing the sick, blessing the children, feeding the hungry, casting out demons, even raising the dead. He met the people at their point of need, and then showed them by his love, his acts of mercy, and his deeds of power the truth of the gospel.

Bob knew that his real mission wasn't to sell swimsuits, but to help people and to enhance their lives by developing a product and selling a product they needed. The central core of our mission in the church is to make disciples of Jesus Christ. The rest of what we do is strategy and tactics for accomplishing this mission.

In what ways have you taken the time to understand the needs of the people you hope to attract to your ministry, program, or church? What are the unmet needs in your community that your church is uniquely suited to meet—needs the meeting of which becomes an expression of the love of Christ, or a means of drawing people to him?

On a recent Saturday night I stopped by the church at ten o'clock to pick up some books I had left in my office, only to find that the parking lot was packed. I thought to myself, "What are all these people doing at the church at ten o'clock at night?" Upon entering the building I followed the sound of music to find four hundred singles dressed in their finest clothes enjoying hors d'oeuvres and fellowship and the music provided by a live band. I was excited to see this. It was part of our strategy to meet the needs of singles in a way that would draw them to Christ. The need the dance sought to meet was fellowship and community. Our singles from the church spent time not only enjoying themselves, but meeting people, and the evening included an invitation for singles who did not have a church home to join our singles for our regular programming and for worship.

This was just one small example of hundreds of similar activities our church is involved in each month. Even the sermons I preach are aimed at understanding the needs of the people we seek to reach. Once or twice a year I preach a series of sermons we call "Fishing Expeditions" (for more information and examples see my book *Unleashing the Word: Preaching with Relevance, Purpose, and Passion* [Abingdon, 2003]). These sermons are announced on Christmas Eve and Easter when we have a large number of unchurched people in worship. The sermons are aimed at piquing the interest of the unchurched, addressing their needs and answering their questions. Recent Fishing Expedition sermon series have included "Where Religion and Science Meet," "Questions Thinking People Ask About the Bible," "Making Love Last a Lifetime," "Where Was God When . . . ," and "Christianity and the Religions of the World."

When I was a youth director we scheduled monthly "Big Events" that were designed to make it easy for our youth to invite their unchurched friends. We offered a terrific Human Sexuality retreat that had unchurched parents sending their teens. We offered occasional classes for parents struggling in conflict with teens. All of these included a spiritual dimension and an invitation for persons to consider being a part of the church.

Among the most creative pastors I have ever met when it came to these kinds of strategies is Steve Sjogren, founding pastor of the Cincinnati Vineyard Church. He took Mother Teresa's famous charge, "Small things done with great love will change the world," and turned it into a strategy for building a significant church. Each week members of his church would meet to go into the community to serve. They would serve shopkeepers in the mall, the urban poor, suburban yuppies, and single moms. When asked by those being served, "Why are you doing this?" the response was typically a very simple, "We want to demonstrate the love of Christ for you in some tangible way."

Bob was excited about his new strategy for bringing together the resources of SecondSkin to meet the needs of the people of the North Slope in Alaska. He was off to a great start.

Questions for Reflection

1. What are the unmet needs that represent real opportunities for your congregation to fulfill Jesus' mandate for you to "love your neighbor" while drawing people to Christ?

2. What does having the "right product" mean when it comes to worship styles? Programming?

3. How else does this chapter speak to your church or ministry?

CHAPTER SIX

Do I Have
the Product *Right*?

B ob and his team from SecondSkin were excited about the challenge and opportunities presented in Barrow. They understood the needs of the customer and were comfortable that they knew the price point they could sell their garments for. And they knew first-hand the weather conditions they would be designing their new line of clothing to be worn in. They went to work, and within a matter of weeks they had successfully designed the prototypes for a line of jogging suits, wetsuits, and exercise wear that would be both comfortable and keep the wearer warm even when the outdoor temperatures reached ten below zero. They sent their samples to Bob, who had selected a test group of twelve men and women from Barrow who agreed to try out these garments every day for one month, reporting back to Bob on their experience. Everyone was excited when the new North Slope Extreme line from SecondSkin arrived.

Bob was certain he had a hit on his hands. He felt a great deal of pride in the garments when he unpacked them, knowing that this line of clothing was his brainchild. He had cast the vision for them, brought together the team of experts, and now had organized the test market. He was sure that once these twelve folks had exercised in and worn the workout suits for a month, they would tell everyone they knew about the comfort and warmth of the North Slope Extreme clothes. He had visions of every person in Barrow lining up at the AC Value Center to *buy the new line. He could see the television commercials: thirty-second spots during next year's Super Bowl showing the people of Barrow raving about North Slope Extreme wear—leading to the greatest product launch of all time.*

Unfortunately, Bob's fantasy proved to be short-lived. Within thirty-six hours he received his first call. Ashley called to report that the inseam of her jogging pants had torn apart, making the pants unwearable. Lightheartedly she asked for her money back. Bob was not amused.

The next day, two more calls came in, this time from Tyler and Susan, who called within minutes of each other. Tyler noted that while the temperature outside that day was a "balmy" 25 degrees, he nearly froze in his new "ultra-warm" jogging suit. Susan wanted Bob to know that she couldn't wear her clothes anymore—they made her itch!

It took less than two weeks for Bob to hear back from each of the members of the test group. No one liked the clothes. They liked the idea of the North Slope Extreme wear, but the implementation left something to be desired. Bob was initially devastated. He took the comments very personally. Were it not for Allison, he might have given up altogether. But she reminded him, "Honey, this is a wonderful thing to have happened—you learned a great deal from these mistakes. Catalog them, carefully evaluate them, and then go back to the drawing board. You have the right idea, it just needs a little work. Don't forget, behind nearly every great product was at least one failure." Bob knew she was right. He had the right idea—the right product—he just didn't yet have the product right.

As a pastor I take criticism of any part of our church very personally. The church is my baby—as the founding pastor of the church I look at it as one of my children. As pastor of a large church, I receive criticism of some aspect of our church's ministry weekly, and at times, daily. Some of it is unfounded, but even that which is unfounded is a learning opportunity.

I recently received a critical e-mail from someone who did not have all of his facts straight. While seeking to offer a caring response, and offering additional information this individual did not have, I also thanked him for writing. What his e-mail told me was that we had not been communicating well with our congregation in a particular area. If this man took the time to write, there had to be a hundred others who would not write but who had the same misconception.

Often the criticism does have merit—there is a log in some aspect of our church's eye—and we are so close to it we cannot see it. Each bit of criticism is a gift that helps us improve.

But we are our own most difficult critics as leaders in the church. Each week we evaluate our worship services to see what went wrong and how we can improve. Every major program in the church is evaluated. Staff members have an annual review that includes input received from their peers, their subordinates, and volunteers who work with them. We set goals for improvement and then monitor to see how we're doing at meeting these goals and objectives.

We are constantly trying to see what we do through the lens of a first-time visitor. We want to know if what we're doing connects with them, or repels them.

My family and I have worshiped at more than one hundred different churches over the last fifteen years when I had the weekend off for vacation or study leave. On a typical weekend off I will worship at three different congregations. When my children were small I would pay them to write up short reports on what they liked and what they didn't like about the children's Sunday schools they would visit. Our family would sit around at lunch and discuss how we experienced the presence of God in worship, and whether we would return to worship in that church again if we were looking for a church home, or if we would not.

Some of these factors are very subjective. But some are, I believe, nearly universal. If the sermon was boring, we found ourselves fidgeting and not interested in returning. If the music was of poor quality it inhibited authentic worship. If the people were unfriendly, or if the liturgy made us feel like outsiders, we agreed we would not be back.

One Sunday we worshiped at one of the country's great cathedrals; I was very excited to worship in this well-known church. Though we arrived early we were seated behind a stone column, obscuring the view of the chancel. This was okay, because the church had installed television monitors for those sitting behind the columns. But as the worship began two things were apparent: the television monitors were not turned on, and the sound system was not working in the back half of the sanctuary. We could neither see what was happening at the chancel, nor could we make out what any of the speakers were saying. We agreed, we would not return to this church. One small detail—a switch turned off on a soundboard—and all of the people in the back half of the sanctuary were left out of the service.

You may have done your homework and know exactly what kind of worship, programs, or ministries would meet the needs or speak to the hearts of the people you hope to attract, but if you fail in the implementation—if you don't get the product right— your efforts will come to naught. So, is your music done well? Is your service accessible? Are your sermons relevant, passionate, biblical, and helpful and do they include excellent illustrations with a touch of humor? Will a visitor find your program worth coming back for, or a waste of time? You must be relentless in your pursuit of an excellent product—it's not enough to have the right idea, you have to implement it well. And this takes practice, hard work, and a willingness to accept, and practice giving, constructive criticism.

Last weekend my wife and I ate at a new restaurant that just opened in our area. It is the ninth Mexican restaurant to open within five miles of our church—great for us, because we love Mexican food. The atmosphere was pleasant. The prices were reasonable. The service was average. The menu was a bit confusing, but we finally figured it out. But as we sat eating our meal we both agreed that the food was just average. It did not have a great deal of flavor, and when compared with the other eight Mexican food eateries, it would rank in the bottom quarter. We agreed that we would not likely be back. In this competitive environment, average food will not sustain a restaurant. I am guessing that by the time you read this book, this new eatery will have made important changes to its recipes, or it will be out of business.

Leonard Sweet once edited a magazine called the *SoulCafe*. I thought this was an appropriate metaphor for the local church, where we are meant to be serving soul food that nourishes the spiritual life of our worshipers. If your church is a soul cafe, how would new patrons rate the service? The atmosphere? The food?

After mulling over the failings of the prototypes of the North Slope Extreme line, Bob began to see opportunity in the failure, and knew that, given another chance, his team could get it right.

The next two months were spent carefully reviewing the comments of each person who had sampled the North Slope line. Conferences were held with the manufacturing plants to incorporate stronger stitching. New specs were submitted for the ultra-warm lining used in the clothes and, in the end, a new supplier was found for these linings. Every inch of the clothing was redesigned from the ground up. This time, before sending the new samples to Bob, SecondSkin decided to test them on employees and paid consultants who were asked to wear the line around the home and office for several weeks to see how they felt, how they held up, and what their experience might be. They even sent their team for an afternoon at the freezer section of a local food wholesaler to measure the warmth of the clothing in sub-freezing temperatures. SecondSkin knew that, before sending out samples for the people to test in Barrow, they needed to be relatively sure they had a quality product. Bob had been very clear when he spoke to his boss at SecondSkin—if his friends in Barrow tried out a second line, and it was fraught with problems like the first, he would not get a third chance with them. And, because people tend to tell their friends of their experiences, Bob told them that a failure here would represent the end of SecondSkin's hopes of providing exercise and sportswear to the people of the Arctic.

Fortunately, this time SecondSkin got it right. All of their hard work, their testing, and their insistence on excellence was evident when Bob opened up the boxes marked "Samples." He delivered his new line to each of his "test consumers" and told them, "This time, I think we've got it right!"

Two weeks later, when his friends came together in the living room of Bob and Allison's small home, they were abuzz. They had never experienced anything quite like these clothes. "I went for a brisk walk each morning—the temperatures were just above zero—and I was sweating when I got home!" "I wore my sweats to my women's reading group. Every lady there asked where they could get a suit like mine—they loved the color and style!" "I found the gloves so comfortable, I won't wear anything else—I can grab my keys, button my coat, and search for change with them on. They're like having on a second skin!" With that everyone had a chuckle. And Bob knew he had a winner!

Questions for Reflection

1. How is your product? Is your worship, ministry, or program done with excellence, or is it simply mediocre?

2. What would a first-time visitor say?

3. What can you do to improve what you are doing? In what ways might you utilize a small group to test your product in order to improve it? How might you use surveys to get valuable feedback?

4. How do you look at criticism? Are you striving for constant improvement?

CHAPTER SEVEN

Embodying the Product: Incarnational Living

W hen Bob and Allison first moved to Barrow, folks were not sure what to make of this couple. Allison they understood. Every year there were a variety of people who came to Barrow to study—scientists who came to study at the Barrow Environmental Observatory or to work with the resources of the Barrow Arctic Research Consortium at the old Naval Arctic Research Laboratory. And, though Allison's work was in the social sciences, the Inupiat had welcomed a long line of people who wanted to study their language and culture. But Bob—Bob was another story. Bob was a salesman, and the people of Barrow weren't sure how they felt about him at first.

So long as Bob saw the people of this town as customers to be sold, or conquered, the people held him at arm's length. Brower's Café, located in the oldest building in the Arctic region—an old whaling station—was Bob's favorite place to go for good food, or just a cup of coffee. But when the guys in Brower's saw him coming, they would quickly finish their coffee to leave. Others just gave Bob the cold shoulder. Salesmen and traveling preachers both left the Brower's regulars with the sense that every conversation always had a hidden agenda—every conversation was a sales pitch.

It is true that this was how Bob looked at the people of Barrow when he first arrived. They represented a challenge. Ultimately their willingness to buy his swimsuits would be a source of validation of Bob's sales *skills—another success story to tell his friends back home. But something began to happen to Bob the longer he lived among these rugged and remarkable people of the North Slope.*

The change started to happen only after Bob's initial realization that he would never successfully sell swimsuits in the Arctic. This had a bit of a humbling effect on this man who had been so certain he could sell anything to anyone. But it was as he was doing his market research for his new brainchild, the North Slope Extreme line of clothing, that the real change began to take place.

Bob's market research had led him to speak with Susan Gnauton, who had been studying the native people of the North Slope for more than five years. He asked her about the needs of the people in this region.

"Bob, to be honest, my primary concern for the native people is for their physical health. There was a day when these were among the healthiest people alive. They worked hard. They ate a diet that came from the land, high in certain kinds of food that provided the perfect nutritional requirements for the people who lived in this rugged place. But today so many of the people, the young people in particular, no longer experience the kind of physical exertion of their forebears. And non-natives have introduced so many processed foods that now make up more than half of the average young person's diet. The results are a tremendous rise in obesity, and with that, increased risk of type 2 diabetes. I am concerned for the people here, but I don't know what to do to help." (While the names are changed, the concern is a real one for the native people of the Arctic, as reported by Patricia Gadsby in "The Inuit Paradox: How Can People Who Gorge on Fat and Rarely See a Vegetable Be Healthier than We Are?" *Discover*, Vol. 25, No. 10, October 2004.)

It was that day that Bob began to look at the people of the North Slope as more than customers. He began, in a way even he didn't understand, to care about them.

Over the weeks that followed, the more he sat down to talk with the people of Barrow, the more he listened to their stories, the more he cared. He came to love these people. Now, it's not that Bob's ego needs, his drive to succeed and make the sale, completely disappeared—but more and more often these drives were overshadowed by his genuine concern for the people.

The people who knew Bob could tell that something was changing in him. Even the guys in Brower's Café warmed up to him and discovered that Bob was a genuinely likeable guy. Instead of talking all the time, Bob would sit and listen as the "fellas" would tell him stories of the whaling traditions of their town, or life before the oil business came to town, or of the days when Alaska was the frontline of the Cold War. The more he listened, the more they talked.

But it was an incident that took place one afternoon, as Bob and Allison walked along the sandy shore of the Arctic Ocean, that would change Bob, and his relationship with the people of this city, forever. On this summer afternoon there were several young children who had taken their father's umiak—the sealskin-covered whaling boats common to the area—out on the water for an adventure. But their adventure quickly turned disastrous as the youngest of the children, a little nine-year-old Inupiat boy, horsing around while standing in the small boat, lost his balance and fell overboard into the 30-degree waters.

Bob's response was instantaneous. Throwing off his coat, he ran into the water, swam to the boy, and pulled him back to shore. He ran with the child in his arms to the nearest home, while Allison called for help.

The child was okay, aside from the scolding he and his brothers received from their father. But before long news had spread of Bob's selfless act, and this was all the townsfolk could talk about for the next forty-eight hours. From that time on those who knew Bob looked at him differently. And Bob, for his part, carried himself differently—not with pride, as one might expect, but with an even deeper sense of love for this community, and a sense of belonging that is seldom experienced by outsiders.

Pastors and church leaders already know the lesson Bob's story teaches—it is cliché but true that people "don't care how much you know, until they know how much you care." In ministry, as in nearly any other kind of venture involving people, few things are more important than building relationships. And meaningful relationships develop when we begin to genuinely care about the other, and give of ourselves to build them up.

Successful pastors are involved in the community, building relationships, getting to know people, encouraging others, finding ways to embody their message. This is, of course, what Jesus did. We know that it wasn't simply what Jesus said that was important, it was also what he did that mattered. He demonstrated his message in the ways he cared for people.

When we care for people, when we listen to them, encourage them, sacrifice something of ourselves for them, we find our hearts changed—we no longer see others simply as potential parishioners, but as friends or people to be loved, and they no longer see us simply as church leaders trying to "save" them, but as real human beings who genuinely care for them.

Growing churches or ministries is all about building relationships and reaching out to care about people. At Church of the Resurrection we've found that advertising for volunteers in our church newsletter and bulletin is the least effective form of recruitment and ministry development. The most effective form of recruitment is when a leader invites her friends to join her in pursuing the ministry together. This is particularly true when this leader has been actively involved in building up and encouraging others.

When we started the church I spent most of my time visiting with people. If I had the choice on a given evening between attending a two-hour committee meeting or visiting two prospective families in their homes, almost always I chose the home visits. I entrusted the committee work to the committee, meeting with the chairs for a monthly lunch meeting to offer my input into their work. Among the most important things I did during the first five years of our church's existence was make doorstop visits, delivering coffee mugs to every first-time visitor to our church. I sought to memorize people's names, to hear their stories, and to be present with them, to the best of my ability, as their pastor.

As the church has grown larger it has become impossible to personally do all of these things, but we try to build systems and ministries to provide "high touch" care for our visitors and members. We don't always succeed, but where we do succeed, we find that people become involved in the church, come to know

Christ, and grow in their faith, ultimately being prepared to serve in ministry on their own through the life of the church.

As pastors, church leaders, and servants in the church, we represent Christ and the church to others. If we are warm, caring, honest, and authentic, others will perceive our church or ministry in this way. If we are cold, aloof, rude, or dishonest, others will associate these characteristics with our congregation, and sometimes, with the Christian faith itself. We must embody the gospel we seek to proclaim.

One last word about this: there are a myriad of small ways in which our churches must embody the gospel. I think of how someone answers the phones at the church. We have had, from time to time, people on the phones at our church who came across as hurried, frantic, or simply unconcerned—they don't generally last long. To a caller who knows nothing else about the church, the voice on the other end of the line is your church, and, at times, is the only picture they will have of Jesus himself.

Likewise your building, your greeters, your signage, your members, and your leaders all point toward the kind of church you hope to be, and your picture of Jesus. How well are you and the leaders or your ministry embodying the gospel? Are you building relationships with those outside your church or ministry?

Bob did not save that nine-year-old boy in order to sell sportswear to the people of Barrow. He did it because he cared. But after he had saved that boy, the townsfolk would, at the very least, listen to Bob talk about anything he might consider selling. He was no longer the obnoxious outsider trying to close a sale—he was one of them, and a man whom they had come to believe genuinely cared about their people. And that would make all the difference.

Questions for Reflection

1. Are you striving to live the faith, or simply talk about it?

2. If all someone knew about your church was what they experienced in an encounter with you, what would they think of your congregation?

3. How do you, or your congregants, embody the message of Christ?

CHAPTER   EIGHT

Selling the "Product"

Selling swimsuits in the Arctic was possible, but only as a curiosity—a gag gift to be worn on the rare summer day. But Bob had been determined to find a product that he could offer the people of Barrow, and the entire Arctic, that would improve the quality of their lives. He found this in active wear—outdoor wear that would be thin and comfortable enough to allow wearers to exercise and pursue activities that would keep them in shape. At the same time it would be warm enough to protect them from the bone-chilling temperatures of the Arctic. But Bob had found that it wasn't enough to have a great idea, the idea needed to be implemented well; he needed a product that actually fulfilled this vision. Ultimately, Bob got his product—a great line of active wear that was revolutionary in its warmth, comfort, and style.

Armed with the right product, and a product that was excellent, there was only one thing left to do: Bob had to actually sell the product. He needed to convince the people of Barrow that his product would, in fact, improve their lives. He needed to help them see why they needed what he was selling. He had to convince them to give SecondSkin's North Slope Extreme line a chance.

He devised three strategies. One was to circulate marketing materials—advertisements in the newspaper, flyers mailed to every home, posters on local bulletin boards, all with a web page that contained more detailed information—in the hope of building awareness of this new product, "Designed, Developed, and Tested Right Here in Barrow, Alaska!" These flyers would include testimonials from his *sample group, who had tested the North Slope line of active wear. Which led to his second strategy: he wanted to enlist his friends who had "field tested" the clothing line, along with a few others in the community, as spokespersons for the line.*

Bob asked his friends to wear their clothing in public whenever possible, and to tell anyone who was interested about their experience with the clothing. He spent time training them, so that they were able to tell the North Slope Extreme story. He gave them a lesson in the exciting new materials that were developed for this line of clothing. He helped them understand the way the lining of the gear pulled moisture away from the skin, how the outer layer was designed of a waterproof and wind resistant synthetic, and how the revolutionary new lining was inspired by NASA's work on the space suit. By the time he was finished, they had a brief lesson in textiles, but more important, they were absolutely convinced that these new clothes were the best thing since sliced bread. Here Bob's strengths as a sales rep shone through. He was able to both inform and inspire the salesmen and saleswomen who worked for him—in this case, his friends who were the first to wear the North Slope line and were commissioned to go tell their friends.

Finally, Bob spent time building relationships with store owners, health workers, school teachers, and anyone else who might have been interested in his new line of clothing, or who might have influenced others to consider trying it out. Bob knew that he was inviting people to make a lifestyle change by exercising, and to try a new product line they had never tried before—and this would require him to personally share the story of North Slope Extreme and SecondSkin with anyone who would listen. This was easy for Bob, because he believed in his product. He knew it was a great product, and he believed that the people of the Arctic, particularly the native populations whose eating and lifestyle patterns had been negatively affected by the immigration of so many outsiders, would see their lives enhanced by what he was selling. He wasn't simply selling clothing, he was selling health. Bob got excited just thinking about his work.

Part of the task of leaders is to inform, inspire, and motivate those they are leading. It is true when you're selling active wear in the Arctic, and it's true when you are seeking to offer Christ to the people in your community. We've got to be clear why people need Christ, why they need the church, and how the lives of others will be positively impacted by becoming Christ's followers and living out their faith in the context of our church.

If you are the pastor of a church, the members of your congregation are your "sales reps," and you might consider that a part of your worship service every week is a sales meeting in which you are training, inspiring, and motivating your sales force. You are teaching them how to talk about their faith, modeling for them how to share Christ, and helping them clearly understand and experience the benefits of following Christ. You provide them with the tools to be able to tell their friends—marketing materials or brochures about your church, CDs or DVDs, or web links for them to find out more, and special events designed to make it easy for them to invite their unchurched friends (see my book *Leading Beyond the Walls* [Abingdon, 2002] for more specific ideas and strategies).

If you are not the pastor, but a leader of a specific ministry, class, or program, you are responsible for doing the same thing for your ministry.

I recently watched two men in our congregation, dads who teach a group of sixth-grade boys in Sunday school, talking about their class. They were so excited about this group of boys and the important things they were doing in this class! They talked about the fellowship and the study these kids did together. They shared with enthusiasm how the boys had raised enough money to help build a small medical clinic in China. They believed that joining their class would be a life-changing experience for any sixth-grade boy. As they were talking about their class, they were selling it to those who were standing nearby. There is no way a parent of a sixth-grader, or any sixth-grade boy, would not have heard their comments and been inspired to actually visit the class.

But our task is not merely to inspire *others* to share Christ, it is to look for creative ways to reach out to others with the gospel ourselves. This may be an awkward thing for some of us to do. Certainly the practice of "witnessing" to others, as we have tra-

ditionally thought of it—folks passing out "tracts" and approach-
ing complete strangers, asking if they are "saved"—is threatening
and something of a turn-off for many of us. But this is not what
sharing Christ has to look like.

I believe the most effective sharing of our faith comes when we
genuinely care about people, when we build relationships with
people, and when we seek to live the gospel. I also believe that
there are many people in our communities who are interested in
spiritual things, if only someone would approach them who was
authentic, caring, and tactful in inviting them to consider the
claims of the gospel. This is where I believe the church, and our
worship services, offers such a wonderful opportunity to share
Christ. The average person will find it difficult to share his or her
faith, but nearly everyone, when excited about their church, can
invite a friend to worship.

One of the things I find interesting in working with people is
that it seems God often brings people into our path, in the hopes
that we will have a spiritual conversation with them, talking
about our "product"—our faith and God's love—with them. The
problem is that we often fail to see it.

Some time back I was on an airplane coming home from a
speaking engagement. I carry a pocket New Testament with me
wherever I go. I was sitting in the aisle seat on the plane reading
one of the epistles. The flight attendant stopped as she was walking by and said, "Looks like you're reading a great book there."
Now, here I could have simply said, "Yes, thanks," and returned
to reading, but aware that sometimes such encounters are more
than coincidences, I looked up and said, "It really is a terrific
book, have you read it?" At this point the flight attendant didn't
know I was a pastor—I was just a passenger reading a pocket New
Testament.

She looked at me and said, "I've tried to read the Bible before,
but it just didn't make any sense." "I understand," I replied. "The
Bible can be hard to understand. But here's what I do: I will read
one chapter at a time. Before I read I pray, 'God, please help me
hear what you want to say to me.' Then I just start reading, looking for at least one verse that speaks to me, or one story that

touches me. I may underline this verse, or I might write a note in the margin. I don't worry about what I don't understand, I just try to find one thing I do understand—and I almost always get something out of it." She said, "That's a great idea, I think I'll try that!"

I then asked her, "Do you go to church anywhere?" She said, "No, I don't. I used to go to church, years ago. But I moved to a new city ten years ago and I haven't been able to find a church I like as well as the one in my hometown that I left." Now, here was a woman who has just told me she is unchurched, and has been so for ten years. She is interested in spiritual things, but she is not connected with a church, not reading the scriptures, and likely missing out on much of the Christian life.

I said to her, "I understand what that's like when you find a church you really love, and then move, and you can't find another one quite like it. Recently a woman I know who had been widowed for twenty years told me that she resisted remarrying for a long time because she could not find anyone just like her first husband. Yet she was lonely and wanted companionship. She finally remarried when she came to realize that she would never find a mate just like her first husband. She stopped comparing men to her first husband and began looking for the good in each man she dated. It was only then that she discovered a new love. It's the same way with a church. Don't try to compare every church with your last one! But it is important to be a part of a church family. It is there that you find Christian friends who can help you grow in your faith, who can pray for you and encourage you. Something happens when you gather in worship—Jesus said that he's present in a special way when two or three gather in his name. You hear the scriptures taught, you receive the sacraments, you grow. Your life would be enriched by being a part of a church family." "I never thought about it that way. I do need to find a new church. Thank you!"

About that time the captain's voice came over the loudspeaker asking the flight attendants to prepare for landing. She returned to her seat. The man sitting next to me said, "That was a great conversation—I enjoyed eavesdropping on it." I responded, "I

enjoyed visiting with her and it is a joy to talk about the faith."
Then I asked him, "Are you involved in a church?" We spent the
next few minutes talking about the faith. Finally, as we were making our final approach, I felt this nudge (a nudge I've come to recognize as the Holy Spirit speaking to me) saying that I was
supposed to give the flight attendant my pocket Testament. I
quickly wrote a note to her in the front page of the Bible. I then
went through the New Testament looking for my favorite passages, dog-earing the pages, and making little notes to her so that
she could have some success in reading passages that would
immediately speak to her.

I waited for the flight attendant to make her way to the front
and said, "I would like to give you my pocket Testament if that
would be okay with you." She looked at me, and said, "You can't
do that. It's your Bible." "I have another," I said, "but I would like
for you to have this one. I have marked some of my favorite passages, and left a note for you in the front. I want you to promise
me you'll find a church when you get home." "I will," she promised, clutching her New Testament. And then I said, "I was
thinking that this Bible is small enough to fit in your purse. If you
were to read it for five minutes at take-off and five minutes at
landing on at least one flight a day for the next year, you would
have finished the entire New Testament. And as you are sitting
there reading, it may be that a passenger might look at you and
say, 'That's an interesting book,' and you might be able to talk
with him about what you are reading, and maybe even give him
this Testament." Her eyes lit up and she smiled, "That would be
really great!"

I left the plane that day feeling a sense of excitement and joy.
There is something wonderful about sharing your faith with people—it makes you feel alive. It was then that I had the idea to
share this story with my congregation, and to give each of them
a pocket Testament. I challenged them to carry it with them at
all times, and to get "caught" reading it. And to look for an
opportunity to give it away to someone who might not have a
Bible. That Sunday in worship we gave every worshiper a pocket
Testament, and invited them to give it away. We promised each

worshiper that we would replace their Testament two additional times, after which they would be on their own to purchase their next Testament.

The response has been exciting—thousands of United Methodists carrying their Bible with them everywhere they go—even our children got in on the act. We've challenged our members to read their Bible daily, to get "caught" reading it, and to give it away. We've had to reorder Bibles twice now! We now give pocket Testaments to every new member of our church.

My point is not to convince you to give away pocket Testaments, but to tell you the importance of personally sharing your faith and looking for opportunities to, with authenticity, gentleness, and love, engage people in spiritual conversations. More than that, it is important for you to realize that leaders model this for their congregations or ministry areas. My telling of this story to the congregation, coupled with equipping them with their own pocket Testaments, has resulted in our members feeling inspired and encouraged to share their faith with others.

Among the most successful marketing strategies we have used at the church is built around candlelight Christmas Eve services. Knowing that unchurched people will come to a candlelight ser-vice, we focus on designing and leading candlelight services that are done with excellence—inspiring, wonderful music, relevant preaching. We then prepare beautiful postcards or mailing pieces that we send to the community to invite them to the services. We then give each of our members these postcards the Sunday before Christmas Eve and invite them to pray for, and then hand deliver, their postcard to a friend who does not have a church home.

On Christmas Eve night we have a huge number of new visitors. In December 2004, just prior to the publication of this book, we had been averaging just over 7,000 per weekend in worship. On Christmas Eve night, over 18,000 people showed up for one of our seven services (we actually began holding Christmas Eve services on the 23rd, inviting our members who were able to attend that night to make room for visitors on the 24th!). On that night, we included a postcard in the bulletin for a new sermon series entitled "Where Science and Religion Meet" (look for this to be published as a small-group curriculum in the spring of 2006). We showed a brief video promo for the series. On the first Sunday of the new sermon series 9,300 people showed up for worship! This told us that we had struck a chord with many unchurched folks who were interested in knowing how to reconcile science and religion. But this response only happened because we had made effective use of marketing, our members had personally invited their friends, and we offered Christmas Eve worship with excellence.

Questions for Reflection

1. How might you model faith sharing for others in your congregation?

2. Are the people in your congregation or program inspired and motivated to share their faith or to invite others to your church or program?

3. When visitors do attend, will they leave wanting to come back?

4. What kind of marketing do you do?

5. What tools do you give your congregation or participants in your program to help them invite their friends?

If at First You Don't Succeed . . .

Having the right product, making sure the product is "right," marketing savvy, and passion can take you a long way toward success in sales and in church leadership—but there is one last attribute that must be mentioned. Successful salespeople, and successful leaders, all share this attribute in common: perseverance.

At least once a week Bob ate lunch at Pepe's North of the Border, a terrific Mexican restaurant that had even been mentioned in The Wall Street Journal *and on* The Tonight Show. *There was nothing like eating Mexican food while in the Arctic! On this particular day Bob arrived at Pepe's with a bounce in his step. He was carrying his suitcase full of samples from the new North Slope Extreme line and he couldn't wait to show them to anyone he knew in the cantina. Having recognized several of the pickup trucks and SUVs parked out front, he was certain he'd be taking his very first order for his revolutionary new active wear. He'd already imagined that he'd frame the check, not even cashing it! This would be a bit of history SecondSkin would want to keep.*

Bob was instantly invited to "pull up a chair" by some of the guys he knew—something he was more than happy to do. "What's in the suitcase, Bob?" "I'm glad you asked! I just happen to have, right here in my suitcase, the most revolutionary line of clothing ever offered this side of space! You guys know I've been working with my company to develop jogging suits, workout clothes, and active wear made especially for the people of Barrow. We've tested it right here on the North Slope. The technology in these babies is straight from NASA. You can jog in them when it's well below freezing. Take a look." And with that, Bob began spreading his wares out on the table.

The guys were all complimentary, and very excited for Bob. They could sense his passion. Finally, Bob spoke up and said, "Okay, guys, I'm taking orders—who wants what? What'll it be?" No one said a word, each waiting for someone else to buy something. The men began to fidget a bit, until finally one of them spoke up and said, "Bob, these things are great, but look at us. Do we look like the 'jogging' types? We've all jogged from our trucks to Fran's place for a healthy helping of her chips and Mexican food! We all think your clothes are great. We know there'll be a lot of people here who want them! Really! It's just that we're not likely to wear them."

"I understand, guys," Bob said, as he began putting the clothes back in his suitcase, "but I'm telling you, if ever there was a group of guys who needed a bit of a workout, it's you! I'm just kidding. But I will tell you, you'd feel a lot better if you'd get out and walk, even three times a week. And you'd look a lot better doing it in these clothes!"

Bob hid his disappointment well, and enjoyed eating with the guys before heading out for his next call. He had forgotten how difficult rejection was, having been out of his normal sales routine for months. But, as a seasoned salesman, he knew that each rejection was an opportunity to learn and to hone his skills. He wanted to remember why these guys said they weren't interested, and he focused on thinking how he could have answered their objections better than he did. He also knew that it takes potential customers some time to begin to accept the idea of a lifestyle change, which was really what he was after—he wanted people to begin taking better care of themselves, and then to wear his product as they did so. It would take more than one attempt to convince people to change their lifestyle habits.

Over the next few weeks Bob took only a handful of orders for his new line of clothing. Each night he would come home to Allison, beginning to wonder if he'd lost his "edge," or if he really was cut out to be in sales, or if he had misread the market, or if his product really wasn't attractive. And each night Allison would encourage Bob, saying, "Remember, Rome wasn't built in a day. Don't give up! You love these people. They love you. It just takes time, and perseverance— keep at it. They'll eventually get it."

Several more weeks went by before Bob finally caught a break. Eleanor called him at home with excitement in her voice. "Bob, I was at my women's circle this morning, telling the ladies about how I'd begun working out—for the first time in years I'm actually walking thirty minutes a day—and how great it feels. And then I told them how it was you who got me to doing it when you asked me to test out the North Slope Extreme line of clothes. They wanted to hear all about it, so I told them how the first attempt at making these clothes didn't go so well, but how hard you worked at this, designing clothes just for the people of Barrow. I showed them mine, and told them everything you told me about how they are made, and they wanted to know if you could come next week and show them the other styles you've got—I think they're really interested. Could you come over?"

Bob could hardly contain his excitement as he put the date and time of Eleanor's women's circle on his calendar. The following week he left Eleanor's home with orders for twelve sets of jogging suits, twelve gloves, twelve scarves, fifteen pairs of socks and three coats! He couldn't believe it! But this was only the beginning. Once the order arrived, these women made a commitment to begin exercising together. The public radio station in Barrow, KBRW, picked up the story and ran it on its morning show, telling not only of this women's circle, but of Bob's work in designing clothing for the North Slope. Suddenly calls began to flood in from people interested in seeing the line. Two local stores asked if they could carry the merchandise. And, perhaps most rewarding of all for Bob, the next time he was in Pepe's three of the guys pulled up a chair at his table, saying that their wives had insisted that it was time they ordered their North Slope gear, because they needed to get in shape!

Over the next five years Bob led a revolution, not only in Barrow, but throughout the Arctic Circle, as people began to get excited about taking better care of themselves. He also led a revolution at SecondSkin. After his success in Barrow, Bob took the North Slope

Extreme line of clothing, and the case for exercising, on the road. He hired local reps around the Arctic Circle. He met with leaders of the Inupiat across the region. And he began making calls in larger markets—beginning in Alaska, then moving across Canada and then the northern United States. What began as a novel project for the company became the largest source of revenue as SecondSkin expanded their revolutionary line of cold weather active wear and even began exporting it around the world. They became the leader in this market segment. But it all started with the vision of one man and his unwillingness to give up.

Those who succeed in business and in the church all have stories to tell of opposition, adversity, and moments when they considered giving up. Many people do give up at the first sign of adversity. Others learn from it, adapt and modify their plans if needed, and keep pressing on.

When we started the Church of the Resurrection, there was opposition—there were people who felt the church should not start in the location I had been assigned. Other neighboring churches saw us as a threat. It would have been easy to throw in the towel, but I felt God had called us to start this church in this place. At nearly every juncture along the way we have had persons, both inside and outside the church, who criticized what we were doing, or who sought to discourage us from moving in this direction or that. But we kept pressing on. If we followed the advice of every naysayer, or if we had been crushed by every unkind e-mail or letter, or if we gave up every time someone threw up a roadblock to the visions or plans we had developed at the church, we would have accomplished very little over the last fifteen years.

I remember when we first made the decision to integrate video into our new sanctuary in 1998. The first month we used the video screens in worship we received six letters from members who complained about the screens and indicated that they would be looking for a new church. We had no one write to express appreciation. I felt discouraged and I worried that we had made a very expensive mistake. I had to go back to the reason why we made the decision to go with video—we felt it was critical as we worshiped in a larger space, we believed it would enhance our ability to communicate the gospel, we felt it would strengthen our congregational singing, and we were certain it would allow us to take worshipers inside our various ministries to inspire them to serve. Remembering these reasons for integrating video in worship, and certain we had made the right decision for the right reasons, we continued to communicate to our congregation our rationale and the purpose of the video screens. Six months later we gave our video team the Sunday off and the screens went black for the day. That week we received a number of complaints from the congregation, upset that we had turned the video off for the weekend! In the end most of the people who left the church over the integration of video ended up returning and today our congregation points to the use of video as a very important part of our ministry.

It is natural to feel like giving up, or giving in, in the face of opposition. Knowing how painful rejection can be, and how discouraging and disappointing criticism and opposition can be, I understand why many give up in the face of these. But the people who succeed—however you define success—are those who are resilient, who persevere, who refuse to give up.

Some years ago my family and I took a summer vacation that included a stop at Mt. Rushmore in South Dakota. I was struck by the amazing feat of artistry and engineering required to create this monument to four American presidents and the values represented by them. There is a museum at the base of the monument that tells the story of Mt. Rushmore, from its initial vision to its financing and construction (which is still incomplete after nearly eighty years). It tells the story of sculptor Gutzon Borglum, who transformed the granite of Mt. Rushmore into what it is today. Borglum had a vision for a sculpture that would forever enshrine the values and character of America. He was supported by people who knew that such a sculpture had the potential to bring millions of visitors to South Dakota (who would, in turn, spend billions of dollars).

But Borglum's vision did not come without its detractors. He was mocked, his vision derided, and his plans called "impossible."

Once he got started he was constantly struggling with collecting enough money to complete the work. While the project began in 1927, it was never fully completed. Borglum spent fourteen years working on it, only six and a half of which were devoted to carving the rock—the rest was spent raising money, answering critics, and garnering support. Borglum died in 1941, but his monument became the symbol not only of the state of South Dakota, but, to many, a symbol of American democracy. True to the hopes of some of his original supporters, his work, which cost one million dollars to construct, today draws more than two million visitors each year who spend hundreds of millions of dollars in South Dakota.

The lesson: Expect adversity, anticipate opposition, and don't give up.

Bob could have given up when he first tried to sell swimsuits in the Arctic. Instead he realized that his mission wasn't to sell swimsuits, but to provide clothing that helped people enjoy the outdoors while enhancing their health. He could have thrown in the towel when his first attempt at designing outerwear for the Arctic failed miserably, but instead he learned from the mistakes and used this as an opportunity to "get it right" the second time. When he finally had the right product, but tried to convince the guys at Pepe's to buy, he was rejected. He could have succumbed to discouragement, but he kept telling the story of North Slope, knowing he had something that would enhance the quality of life for the people of Barrow. Finally, his perseverance paid off.

Questions for Reflection

1. How have you faced adversity or opposition in your work as a leader? What lessons have you learned from it?

2. People are naturally resistant to change. If you propose doing ministry in a new way, which you will likely have to do if you are going to reach a new generation of people, this will require

change. What kind of opposition do you think you might face? What can you learn from Bob's approach to rejection, adversity, and disappointment that might help you persevere?

3. When it comes to inviting people to church, or marketing to your community, what lessons are to be learned from Bob's first attempts to market the North Slope Extreme line to the people of Barrow?

CHAPTER TEN
Concluding Thoughts

L et's wrap up this little book with a final look at what
we've learned from Bob's efforts at selling swimsuits in the
Arctic.

We learned that much of what we do in life is "sales"—and
this is particularly true in the church. Sales involves persuasion
and motivation. I am reminded of the apostle Paul's words in
2 Corinthians 5:20, where he writes, "So we are ambassadors for
Christ, since God is making his appeal through us." God makes
his appeal through us, which involves the art of persuasion and
motivation—sales. And when Jesus gave the great commission,
commanding his followers to "Go therefore and make disciples of
all nations, baptizing them in the name of the Father and of the
Son and of the Holy Spirit, and teaching them to obey everything that I have commanded you" (Matthew 28:19-20), he was
asking us to do something that would involve selling. Making disciples involves the art of persuasion. Many of the same attributes
that make one an excellent salesperson are needed to be an
excellent leader in the church. That was the premise of this book.
From there we studied seven simple keys to success in sales. Keys
modeled for us by our friend Bob are:

1. We must believe in our product.
2. We must believe that others need what we're selling.
3. We must understand the needs of those we're seeking to reach.

4. We must offer an excellent product or service.
5. We must embody the values and ideals of our product.
6. We must effectively market the product.
7. We must not give up in the face of adversity or rejection.

Bob lived these keys, and he was ultimately successful at what he did. Each of these keys has a direct application for every church leader, in every ministry area within the church, and for every congregation. Growing churches live these keys, even if they don't think of them in sales and marketing terms.

But there are two final lessons I want you to notice from Bob's story. These were implicit but not explicit. I wonder, did you catch them?

The first was a change that happened in Bob. It was subtle, and was not ever completed—he was always in process regarding this transformation. What was this change? It was the change from serving himself to serving others. Bob came to Barrow with dreams of selling swimsuits in the Arctic. He knew up front that the Inupiat of Barrow did not need swimsuits, but they represented a challenge—an opportunity to prove his prowess at sales. If he could sell swimsuits in the Arctic, he could sell swimsuits anywhere. He didn't realize it, but his efforts were all about personal ambition and meeting his ego needs. But over time, Bob began to have a change of heart. He began to care about the people of Barrow. He began to be concerned about their needs. He became interested in what was in their best interests. It's important to note that this transformation was not completed in this book. Bob continued to be motivated, at least in part, by his own ego needs. But he seemed to put the needs of others before his own need for affirmation and success, and he allowed the latter needs to motivate his pursuit of the health and welfare of the Inupiat of the Arctic.

Successful church leaders are aware of their own ego needs, but seek to place the needs of others first. Again the apostle Paul speaks to this when he writes in Philippians 2:3-4, "Do nothing from selfish ambition or conceit, but in humility regard others as better than yourselves. Let each of you look not to your own interests, but to the interests of others." This is what sanctification in the Christian life looks like. It is loving God wholly and completely, and loving our neighbors as we love ourselves. This is the foundation of excellent Christian leadership: recognizing that our primary aim is to please God, and closely related to this is God's desire that we love people.

The second thing I hope you noticed about Bob was what happened when he came to see that those in the Arctic didn't need swimsuits. He could very easily have thrown in the towel, left SecondSkin, and taken up a new vocation. But he didn't do this. Instead he took the time to get to know the people in the Arctic, carefully considered their needs, and then he began to brainstorm about how his company could fulfill its mission while addressing the needs of the people of Barrow. It was here that he *saw* an idea; he saw something that as yet did not exist—he had a *vision*. His vision was of a line of clothing that would actually encourage people to take better care of themselves—a line of clothing that would enhance the lives of the people.

We speak of what Bob displayed as "visionary leadership"—the capacity to develop new ideas and new plans that link together the needs of the community with the resources of the organization, and then to align the resources to achieve the vision. Some people are born with a wonderful intuitive ability to see what others cannot see. You likely have some of those people in your church. You yourself may be such a person. But even if you don't see yourself as a visionary, you can, with God's help, develop visions. And the success of your church or ministry likely depends upon it.

Begin by remembering the purpose or mission of your church or particular ministry. Why does this ministry or church exist? Next, take a careful inventory of the resources available to your ministry, program, or church. You likely have people who can give their time in service to Christ and others. You probably have a building that is underutilized at certain times of the week. You have some financial resources—even if just a small amount. In addition you may have the resource of influence over others. Next, make a careful assessment of the needs of the people in your church and especially of those outside of your church, those you are seeking to reach. Now spend time in prayer, inviting God to help you see how you might fulfill your mission by meeting the needs of the community using the resources at your disposal. You may begin to see new visions on your own, but the wise church leaders will pull together a team of people in the church to do this work, together seeking God's visions for the congregation.

This is an exciting and exhilarating experience—dreaming of what God could do through you to positively affect others. I think about the folks in my church who are involved in our computer ministry. These men and women love computers. They have the ability to repair computers. They know how to teach others to use computers. And some of them work for large companies in the IT departments. They know that part of our vision at the church is to transform our community. So they began looking for ways that they could use their time, talents, and the resources of our church to fulfill our vision through computers. They set up a computer lab using donated computers to teach senior adults how to use the Internet. They created a ministry in which students with disabilities from the local high school could do their vocational training at our church, learning data entry while experiencing the love of our congregation members. They invited congregation members to donate used computers that could be rehabbed and upgraded and then donated to inner-city mission agencies and churches that did not have computers. Most of these men and women would not think of themselves as "visionary leaders"—just men and women open to what God could do through them. And God has used them in profound ways.

This is only one example out of hundreds in our church. People are excited by compelling visions of what could be, and how they could use their gifts and abilities to make a difference for Christ. The older translations of Proverbs 29:18a note, "Without a vision the people perish." My experience is that people and congregations have no sense of purpose or direction when there is no vision. When Bob determined that selling swimsuits in the Arctic was a losing proposition, he set about searching for a new vision for his life. When he hit on the vision of healthier people through exercise, made possible by a new line of exercise clothing his company could manufacture, he found a new zeal and renewed sense of passion.

But what if Bob had simply given up on his first vision without ever pursuing a new vision? Many of our churches are like this—we keep doing the same things we've always done, but we lost our vision long ago, and consequently we've lost our sense of purpose, focus, and direction. Our people have no motivation to give of their time, talent, and resources. They have no "preferred picture of the future"—instead, like hamsters running in their wheels, never going anywhere, busily running in place, our congregations look longingly at the past, when there was an excitement, or they become inwardly focused in the present, finding a certain comfort in simply caring for one another as a ward of sick patients might do as they await death.

This is not the future God desires for your church! By now you know that my aim in telling you Bob's story had nothing to do with selling clothing to the people of Barrow, but everything to do with helping you remember the fundamental principles of excellent leadership, and then inviting you to look for ways that the resources of your church can address the real needs of people in your community such that you are leading people to Christ, bearing witness to his love, and seeing your own lives transformed in the process. And these are the lessons we learn from a man who thought he wanted to sell swimsuits in the Arctic.